CELEBRATING THE TRIDUUM

Eugene Duffy, Siobhán Garrigan, Celia Hayes,
Patricia Lynott, Enda Lyons, Francis McMyler

Celebrating the Triduum

Edited by
Eugene Duffy & Enda Lyons

the columba press

First published in 1999 by
the columba press
55a Spruce Avenue, Stillorgan Industrial Park, Blackrock,
Co Dublin

Cover by Bill Bolger
Origination by The Columba Press
Printed in Ireland by ColourBooks Ltd, Dublin

ISBN 1 85607 256 8

Acknowledgements
Much of *Deepening our Appreciation for Eucharist* by
Eugene Duffy first appeared as an article in *Priests and
People* in June 1998.

Contents

PART III: HOLY THURSDAY

Preface

The chapters of this book were first presented as papers at seminars over three weeks in Lent 1998 for parish teams of the dioceses of the Tuam Province in the West of Ireland. The seminars were a project of the Western Theological Institute, 16 University Road, Galway, and the overall director of the project was Fr Eugene Duffy.

There is some duplication, perhaps repetition, in the chapters on the actual celebration of the Triduum. We have decided, however, to leave these as each of the contributors brings her suggestions independently and out of her own background. Whatever repetition is there will serve to strengthen the suggestions.

The contributors to the original workshops would like to acknowledge the helpful suggestions and comments offered by Sr Patricia Holden SHCJ on ritual and music. Our thanks also to Fr Paul Kenny for his help with sources.

The Editors
27 January 1999

A Word About Ritual

Enda Lyons

The last three days of Holy Week are, of course, the high point of the Christian liturgical year. Naturally they are celebrated with an abundance of ritual. Anyone hoping to do justice to the liturgy of these days needs to have an understanding of ritual and a feel for it.

Ritual: a feature of life

We who are involved in liturgy sometimes seem embarrassed by ritual, feeling that it is altogether 'out of this world' and found only in church life. We need to get over this embarrassment and realise that ritual is a very common and important feature of life generally. Christmas, even as a purely secular feast and in its secular celebration, is altogether surrounded by ritual: there are, for example, the multi-coloured lights, the holly, the exchange of cards, the verbal greetings and the gifts, the Christmas crackers and the candles, the traditional songs and even the traditional foods. Birthdays and other anniversaries also have their ritual – the party or the meal out, and again the cards, the presents and the traditional birthday song in which everybody joins. Our All-Ireland Final Day has wonderful ritual without which it would not be the same: there is the great sea of colour, the chants and songs, the parade of the band and the teams, the arrival of the President, the speeches, and the inevitable 'hip-hips' for the losers. The use of ritual seems, if anything, to be on the increase today.

Mother's Day and Father's Day, with their own rituals of flowers and cards and gifts, seem relatively new to the Irish scene. The Deb's Dance at the end of the school year – she with her special dress and he, with his new bow tie, bringing the 'traditional' rose and box of chocolates – certainly did not exist here in my school days.

Occasions for ritual

In preparing to make the best use of the rituals provided by the liturgy of Holy Week it will help if we reflect on the occasions in life in which we tend particularly to use rituals. These, we find, are occasions in which there is a depth of meaning and significance for the individual and the community involved. The birth of a child, always celebrated with ritual in every culture, is unsurpassable in its significance both for the newly born child and for the community into which this new member is born. So too is the death of a person. The marriage of two people, marking the formal setting up of a new family unit, which again is universally celebrated with ritual, is an event of profound significance for the couple and for the community. Graduation, celebrated with the ritual academic gown and the presentation of the parchment, marks the highly significant occasion of the end of one's student days and the beginning of one's professional life. The twenty-first birthday, with the symbolic key, still seems to be celebrated as that significant moment when one leaves home and enters, in one's own right, the adult world.

The ingredients of ritual

Recalling the occasions for ritual helps us to note its ingredients. These are many. They are not just words and story. They are also the colour and the music and the song and the movement of, for example, an All-Ireland Day or a St

Patrick's Day, the dress of a Graduation ceremony, of a Deb's dance or of a special evening-out, the lights of Christmas and the candles of an anniversary dinner table.

The purpose of ritual

Noting the ingredients of ritual helps us to see its purpose. Its purpose is to draw our attention to the full significance of the occasion in question and to unpack for us its many layers of meaning – to draw our attention, for example, to the depth of meaning of a birth or a death, to open our eyes to the full significance of the event of setting up a new family unit, or to help us to marvel at the achievement, the determination and the commitment of the fifteen or so young men who, coming from their native county, have now become the champions of the whole country. In opening up for us the depth of meaning of the event we are marking, ritual also draws us ever more deeply into this event. And in doing this it gives us a deeper sense of unity with all those with whom we share this ritual celebration. How deeply could we really enter into that All-Ireland event, or how closely would we really feel united with those around us, without any of the ritual?

The technique of ritual

How does ritual achieve its purpose? Its technique is to appeal to and engage all our senses and, so, involve the whole person. The full human significance of a birth – or of a death or a marriage – cannot be brought home to those immediately involved simply by their being told about it. It is only when all our senses are engaged – our eyes to see it, our ears to hear it, our feeling to touch it, our scent to smell it, our taste to savour it – that we can be brought to experience the event in all its dimensions and be drawn fully into it.

Doing it well

Planners of the Holy Week liturgies have no need whatsoever to be ill-at-ease with or embarrassed by having to deal with ritual. What ought, perhaps, to worry them is a failure to appreciate ritual or to use it properly. For if there is one thing which needs to be remembered about ritual it is that if it is to be used at all it needs to be used properly. To be serious about ritual is to be serious about doing everything possible that will help to draw people into the event which is being celebrated.

Questions to be asked by planners

Three questions need, then, to be asked before we begin to plan the three great liturgies of Holy Week:

1. What meaning is to be unpacked here and into which we hope to draw a congregation?

2. What rituals are provided and available for unpacking this depth of meaning?

3. How can the power of these rituals be effectively released?

These questions need to be asked first about the Triduum as a whole and then about each of its three parts – Holy Thursday, Good Friday and Easter Vigil.

Easter – Planning the Liturgy

Siobhán Garrigan

Liturgy and the Local Context

The workshops that gave rise to this book were designed with people living in the west of Ireland in mind, and many of the technical aspects of the liturgy that we discussed were tailored to meet the specific needs of this locality's churches. At the heart of all good liturgy is an awareness of local traditions, needs and desires, and thus it is impossible to write in a generalised way about what a particular liturgy in a particular place might include.

All that follows is therefore offered as a trigger to your own imagination, to encourage you in thinking about how to celebrate Easter in your own community. The ideas and examples given are not blueprints, and will not work if taken straight off the page and imposed on the Easter missalettes. They all require digestion, discussion, adaptation and maturation before they will fulfil all you would like them to.

In trying to do anything new or different in a church, it is essential to be aware that you *are* doing something new or different. It may sound obvious, but it is often overlooked. There is a well-worn saying, 'Start from where you are at' meaning, take full account of the status quo and use it as your starting point. Remember that any departure from this, no matter how slight, is going to represent a big change for many participants.

Start where your community is at, but don't stop there!
Being aware of the status quo and being brow-beaten by it
are two entirely diffferent things. All too often, 'This is the
way we have always done it' is used to avoid the uncomfortable issues raised by doing something differently
rather than because it is actually the best possible way of
doing it now. Most people are resistant to change, especially
in something as important to them as the liturgy, but the
same people also have the capacity to embrace change and
be delighted and empowered by what it brings them – it
all depends on how you handle it.

A good starting place is to form a group that will discuss
the liturgy. Within this group, begin by asking what you
would like the liturgy in your church to do that it is not
doing. Discuss your own local customs and traditional
ways of doing things and highlight those that work, those
that you can build on. Ask why you are considering new
approaches and what you hope these will achieve. After
your discussion, tell as many other church members as
possible about what was said, including any differences of
opinion. By sharing your reasons for introducing new
ideas or developing exisiting ones, you will avoid the per-
ception of 'change for change's sake' and also, more im-
portantly, you will bring as many people as possible along
with you.

Short, Mid and Long Term Changes
If most of the suggestions given below are new to you, do
not try to use all of them this year. In fact I would recom-
mend introducing only one or two variations per night.
Many of the suggestions require a great deal of planning
before they can be succesfully carried out. If there is an
idea that you like, but feel would be too complex to try,

then set it as a goal for next year, or for five years hence, and make a decision to work towards being able to do it then.

For example, the proposal that 'communion should be wine as well as bread' is obviously not going to be feasible at a moment's notice if it is not already your custom. In addition to the discussion such a big change may require, you will need to train and commission eucharistic ministers, buy chalices, let the congregation know how it will work and how to receive the chalice, not to mention buying a lot more wine! I would therefore suggest that if you can't do it this year, adopt it as an aim for the parish and spend the coming year preparing so that you can have wine as well as bread from next Easter onwards.

The suggestions offered below are by no means an exhaustive list of all that could be done on the Easter weekend. Many congregations have tried many more adventurous things with great success. I have concentrated on ideas for 'middle of the road' parishes. Not that there is anything 'middle of the road' about the activity of the Spirit in the church – on the contrary! All I mean is that if your church has encountered Vatican II in little other than use of the vernacular, then these suggestions will seem radical; if your church is used to engaging all one's senses and including all its members in imaginative ways, then what follows will seem sedate.

Every idea I mention is an example, not a template. Each suggestion has been used by a worshiping community, most of them Roman Catholic churches in Ireland. They are examples of how certain communities have interpreted the various aspects of the liturgy to suit their own needs and they are no doubt being developed, adapted and discarded as I write. You are invited to do the same.

As liturgical ministers, whether we are musicians, cantors, readers, altar servers, presiders, flower arrangers, welcomers, critics, sacristans or one of many other roles, our task is to enable the participation of the congregation in the reality of Easter.

Cutting Your Cloth

The Easter Triduum involves a rich wealth of symbols, stories and sacraments. It is just not possible to give equal weight to all aspects each year. Many parishes therefore choose to slightly emphasise a particular one each year (or for a series of years). However, a balancing act is needed between exploring one element in depth and not ignoring any of the others. For example, the Easter Vigil, one of the most glorious feasts in the church's year, can not be reduced to a 'theme mass' on the *Exodus*. All the 'themes' have to be present, have to be lived, as they all inform each other and work together to transform us.

Think about what your community needs this year, and tailor the elements of the liturgy to meet these needs. For example: would you benefit from some time reflecting on the idea of service (develop the washing of the feet ritual); has there been a lot of suffering this past year (work on a meditation on the cross); are there personal divisions that need reconciliation or healing (fire-building/prayer boards/cross-carrying). The liturgy was made for humans, not humans for the liturgy, so make it work for you!

All God's Creatures Have a Place in the Choir

People have to feel included in the liturgy before they can feel the ownership of it that is necessary if they are to participate fully in it. As liturgical ministers, we have to engage all the senses of every participant. If people's sight, hearing,

taste, smell, touch and intuition are aroused, they are involved. All too often, worship can be reduced to words in a
Missal, words on a hymn sheet, words from the priest. The
Easter Triduum is a great opportunity to rediscover how the
liturgy involves the participation of the whole person.

The liturgy was made for all humans, but in reality some
people are often excluded. For example, some who are
young and small cannot see what is going on; some who
are older feel that their ways of worshipping have been
destroyed; some are disabled and get stuck at the back or
can't move up the aisle for communion; others can't read
and therefore can't follow written prayers or hymns; some
are offended by exclusively male language (calling God
'he'); yet others are excluded by virtue of their sexuality or
marital status preventing them from being in full communion with the rest of the community.

You will not be able to consider all of the above in one go,
but there are many, many things you can do as a start (and
some examples are given below). The most important is to
be aware of how you could be more inclusive.

Easter is a good time to contact parishioners who have
stopped going to church, and ask them why (and if you
make changes on the basis of their recommendations, invite them back too). It is not easy for churches to face these
issues. They can be very painful and threatening for all
concerned. But you have to trust in the work of the Spirit,
and pray that the Spirit will guide you through. It will be
worth the risks involved.

PART I

The Easter Vigil

The Easter Vigil
– a theological note

Enda Lyons

In the actual celebration of the three great days of Holy Week the Easter Vigil, of course, comes last. But though Easter comes last in time it comes first in significance. It is from Easter that Good Friday gets its full Christian meaning. Without Easter, Good Friday would not mark the death of the Risen One. Apart from Easter, Good Friday would literally have been a dead end. It is from Easter that Holy Thursday too derives its full Christian significance. Without the Risen Christ of Easter, there would have been no church, no Eucharist. The Last Supper would really have been a last. Because the full meaning of the liturgies of Holy Thursday and Good Friday can be appreciated only when seen in the light of Easter, it seems appropriate to begin our reflections on Holy Week by exploring the meaning of Easter itself and of the Easter Vigil.

Following on what has been said earlier in the context of ritual, the three questions which need to be asked about the Easter Vigil are:

1. What, in all its richness of meaning, is being celebrated here, what is this Easter event into which we hope to be drawn?

2. What rituals are provided and available to draw us into this event?

3. How can the power of these rituals be most effectively released?

This chapter will discuss the first two of these questions; different aspects of the third will be discussed in the three chapters which follow.

1. What Easter Celebrates

1. The Resurrection of Jesus

Easter obviously has to do first of all with Jesus himself. It marks his resurrection. How we talk about Jesus' resurrection is important as it affects how we think about it and understand it. To speak about Jesus rising from the dead (as indeed scripture sometimes does) is not always the most helpful way. For one thing it might give us the impression that somehow Jesus, being able to rise again by his own human power, did not really die. A more helpful way of talking about it, especially in our present context, because it gives us a better understanding of what is being celebrated at Easter, is to use the language of, for example, the Acts of the Apostles. This speaks of the resurrection of Jesus in terms of God bringing Jesus, one of ourselves, through death to a new and glorious kind of life. This, for example, is the way Peter is presented as speaking of the resurrection on the first Pentecost:

> Then Peter stood up with the Eleven and addressed them in a loud voice: 'Men of Israel, listen to what I am going to say: Jesus the Nazarine was a man commended to you by God by the miracles and portents and signs that God worked through him when he was among you, as you all know. This man ... took and had crucified ... You killed him, but God raised him to life, freeing him from the pangs of hades ... Now raised to the heights by God's right hand, he has received from the Father the Holy Spirit ...' (Acts 2:14, 22, 23, 32, 33; see also Acts 5:31; 13:32; Rom 1:3-4; Phil 2:8-11).

Expressed in these terms, the Christian conviction about the resurrection of Jesus is that even though Jesus died – really died, 'died and was buried', 'descended into the realm of the dead' – he did not end in death. God brought him through death to eternal life. The resurrection of Jesus does not mean that Jesus was brought back, Lazarus style, to this life. Jesus, in his death, 'departed this life' in the usual sense of that phrase. His resurrection means that his life and death were so approved by God, his Father, that he who lived and died was brought by God, through death, into the divine sphere, 'seated at God's right hand', where he is Lord and Christ (Acts 2:36).

2. Our Liberation

What is celebrated at Easter is, in the second place, our liberation. For we are indeed in need of liberation. Our lives are under great threat. There is, for example, the ever-present destructive power of sin. If we understand sin properly we can see that it is a truly destructive power. Sin is misunderstood if it is seen simply as the violation of a law imposed on us by God, or by the church, just to test our obedience. One of the most common words which the Bible uses for sin, the Greek word *hamartia*, gives us a clue to sin's true meaning and an insight into its destructiveness. *Hamartia* is a word associated with archery and it means missing the target. Sin only really occurs when we knowingly and willingly go off-target in the way we live our lives and so cease to live authentically. Sin is a destructive force in our lives because there is always that powerful temptation to take the soft option and so to fail to be true to our real selves, to others and to God.

Along with sin there is, of course, that final and fatal threat to our lives – death. Death, with its apparent finality, threatens to consign us finally to darkness, the empty darkness of the tomb. So it threatens to frustrate and render ultimately futile all our deepest hopes and noblest desires.

Easter celebrates our liberation as well as – or, rather, in – that of Jesus because Christian faith does not see Jesus as just an individual human being. Christian faith sees him as a representative of all humanity, as in a sense embodying the race. It sees in the victory which God gave Jesus over sin and death a pledge and guarantee of the ultimate victory which God will give the race over sin and death. In the words of scripture, Christian faith sees the Risen Jesus as 'the first to rise from the dead' (Acts 26:23), 'the first to be born from the dead' (Col 1:18; Apoc 5), or, as St Paul put it: '... the first-fruits of all who have fallen asleep' (1 Cor 15:20).

> Death is swallowed up in victory. Death, where is your victory? Death where is your sting? Now the sting of death is sin, and sin gets its power from the Law. So let us thank God for giving us the victory through our Lord Jesus Christ (1 Cor 15:55-56).

3. The Power of the Risen Christ Today

The power of God manifested in the resurrection of Jesus ought not to be seen just as belonging to the past. The power of the Risen Christ is present in our own lives and in our world. The Easter celebration invites us to open our eyes to this presence. This is a point which Seamus O'Connell has expressed simply and well:

> When we come to Easter, we run one risk more than all others: we run the risk of placing Easter in the past. We go back into the past, just like the women who went to the tomb. But just as they could not find Jesus in the tomb, we cannot find him in the past because he no longer lives in the past.

Why do we look in the past for one who is alive, for one who lives right now? … the men in brilliant clothes still call to us, will challenge us to open our eyes, no longer to look for the Living One among the dead. So look around you this Easter Night (Morning) and seek the signs of the Living One.

… the power of the Risen One … is here and it is active. Even in our battered and bruised and half dead church, the power of the Risen One is still here. He still brings mourners joy, he still casts out hatred, in all our turmoil he brings some peace. That's the power of the one who is alive and alive now …Look in the present and see the signs … (Homily: Easter, in *The Furrow,* March 1998).

Easter, then, has to do with the victorious presence of God in our history. In the liturgy of Christmas we celebrated the *radical and irreversible* quality of God's involvement in our history: for there we celebrated the Eternal Word of God, in the incarnation, becoming one of us and so entering our history at its very roots *(radix)* and, taking our history to the divine Self in a way that can never be undone – for the Word can never un-become flesh. At Easter we are invited to focus on and celebrate the *ultimately victorious* nature of this divine involvement in our lives and in our history. Easter assures us of the ultimate validity of all our human hoping. It tells us that we have every reason to be hoping even against hope, that we should not at all be surprised that hope springs eternal in the human mind for, in the words of St Paul,

With God on our side who can be against us? (Rom 5:31).

2. What Rituals are Provided and Available?

The Easter event touches our very deepest hopes and so has a great depth of human meaning. We can hardly be surprised to find that an abundance of ritual is provided for this celebration. Nor should we be surprised to find that all the ingredients of ritual, mentioned in the introduction, are found here. What we do need to keep constantly in mind is the purpose of all this ritual: its purpose always is to open up for us the full meaning of the event which is being celebrated and to draw us as deeply as possible into it.

There are, in all, four festivals in the Easter Vigil:
– The Festival of Light
– The Festival of Story
– The Festival of Water
– The Festival of Thanks (the Eucharist).

The Festival of Light
We can hardly think of anything which could unfold the meaning of the resurrection and draw us more deeply into this liberating event than the experience of light, of brilliant light. We cannot, however, appreciate light without experiencing – even savouring – darkness. This is the twofold experience, of darkness and of light, that the Festival of Light offers us and invites us to enter into.

The Festival of Light begins, as it has to, with an experience of darkness, of the physical darkness of night itself which helps us to enter into and, again, even savour, the dark side of our lives, of our world and of our unredeemed hopes. Out of this darkness light, slowly but steadfastly, comes. It comes first from the dark earth to the Paschal Fire. From the Fire it comes to the Paschal Candle, that

great Easter symbol of the Risen Christ. The lighted candle, big and bright and strong, moves slowly – perhaps
very slowly – through a darkened church, a darkened
world. It gradually breaks through the darkness and illu-
minates the world as each person present personally part-
icipates in, and even grasps, his or her own candle lit from
the Christ Light. After illuminating the whole church, the
Christ candle is enthroned in full view of everyone, is
solemnly reverenced, incensed and, finally, serenaded in
the great Easter Hymn, the Exultet. The joy in the resurrection voiced in this hymn is so great and so exuberant that
gratitude is expressed even for our experience of sin – for
without this we would not experience our liberation:

O happy fault, O necessary sin of Adam,
which gained for us so great a Redeemer!

So much of our life, of what is deepest in us, is touched on
in the Easter Vigil that all the ingredients of ritual are employed – darkness and light, of course, but also movement,
song, the feel of one's own personal candle with its light,
the scent of the incense, the colour of, for example, the
flowers visible when the Light has filled the whole church.
There is, on this night, a great event into which we are to be
drawn. There is a great power of ritual to draw us into it.

The Festival Story
For believers Easter night is surely a night for stories. It is a
night for recalling, for remembering, for reliving. It is a
night for the Christian family to sit around the fire and tell
again and hear again the great stories of their past – stories
which do not just belong to the past but which are relevant
to and can become real in the present. It is, in the old Irish
tradition, a Christian *oíche cois teallaigh (night by the fire-
side).*

The stories prescribed or suggested by the liturgy books are many (nine in all) and they are interspersed with songs and psalms and prayers. Their number, however, ought not to cause us to forget their main thrust. It would be wrong to try to fit them, over-neatly, into a single theme. However, if we were to attempt to do that, the overall theme which would emerge would undoubtedly be that of God's powerful and liberating presence in our lives and in the world. This is clearly the theme of the following three main stories.

The first story which is retold is one of the biblical stories of creation. This, however, is not at all an account of creation, but rather a hymn of creation and a hymn to God's majestic and powerful presence in the process, even the ongoing process, of creation.

The Exodus story has many layers of meaning. At its surface level it recalls how God, through Moses, freed the Israelites from the slavery of Egypt and brought them, through water, to the freedom of the Promised Land. At another level it tells of how God, through Jesus, frees us from the slavery of sin and death and brings us, through the waters of baptism, to the freedom of the children of God – to a large extent it was in terms of this story that the first Christians interpreted and expressed what God had done in the death and resurrection of Jesus. At yet another level the story tells of the liberating presence of God in our own lives and in today's world – the story of how God, through so many human agents, can, and does, still free us from, for example, the slavery of alcoholism, drugs, hatred and jealousy, and lead us to a more free and authentic life.

The first reading from the Christian scriptures, a reading

from St Paul, stresses our participation, through baptism, in God's liberating act in Christ. It assures us that:

> If in union with Christ we have imitated his death we shall also imitate him in his resurrection (Rom 6:5-6).

The story from the gospels emphasises that Jesus, though dead, is to be found not among the dead but among the living.

In planning this Festival of Story the danger to be avoided is that of forgetting the point of telling them. The point is not by any means to bore. On the contrary, it is to do what all ritual strives to do, that is, to draw us ever more deeply into the events being recalled. The Easter Vigil's Festival of Story presents a special challenge to a liturgy team. Some help in this area will be given in three chapters which follow.

The Festival of Water

For drawing us into the light-giving event which Easter celebrates, the symbol of water could hardly be overlooked. Water has a freshness. It is life-giving and life-restoring. It cleanses and renews. It has important Christian associations, more notably baptismal ones. It is not at all surprising that one of the four major festivals of the Easter Vigil is a festival of water, especially of baptismal water.

It is interesting to note how this festival begins: it begins with a solemn invocation of the whole company of the great Christian saints, asking them by name, one after another, to be present with us with their prayers at this solemn festival.

This Litany is followed by the Blessing of the Water. Here all the happy memories of water in Christian history are recalled:
– water as the womb of life in the Genesis story,
– water as purifying and cleansing human life in the Flood,
– water as the passage from slavery to freedom in the Exodus,
– water of the Jordan in which Jesus was baptised by John,
– water as our passage to newness of life in baptism.

For all these happy memories God is thanked. This blessing of the Easter Water is nothing less than *A Christian Ode to Water*. Again there is need to remember the purpose of this Festival of Water. Its purpose is to draw us into that newness of life which we are celebrating at this Vigil. As with all ritual, it seeks to achieve that purpose by engaging all the senses. We are meant, then, to see the water, to feel it and be blessed by it. Perhaps we can manage even to hear it – but suggestions such as this will be made in the following chapters.

The climax of this Festival of Water is, as we might expect, a baptism when at all possible, and a solemn renewal of baptism.

The Festival of Thanks – the Easter Eucharist
The Easter Vigil culminates in the celebration of the Eucharist. The Mass is always a festival of thanks, for that is what the word Eucharist means. When planning the Easter Eucharist we might perhaps keep in mind the words of the Preface of that Vigil:

'We praise you *with greater joy than ever* on this Easter night' (emphasis mine).

Easter Vigil: A Living Liturgy

Siobhán Garrigan

General Guidelines

Many aspects of this evening's liturgy will feel unfamiliar to the regular Sunday congregation. It is important to enable everyone to be involved and to feel comfortable.

At a very simple level, think of the space people enter when they come into the church. Flowers, low lighting and symbolic objects (more later) all help set the tone and provide focal points for the participants as they settle into the worship environment, as does music.

If there is no organ or choir, use taped music to provide a meditative atmosphere at this gathering time. The music should be light, not sombre.

If you have produced a missalette for the evening, why not have a couple of 'welcomers' on the door to give it out personally and say hello to people at the same time. It is important to feel welcome, because only then can we make the liturgy our own, so the church should feel hospitable.

This evening's liturgy is dense with symbols. The challenge is to describe and explain them without killing them by over-explaining. Symbols 'speak' for themselves, but some of them also benefit from a careful word or two explaining their history in this liturgy.

With the lighting of the candles for example, explaining the significance of the light spreading from our common baptismal symbol, the Paschal Candle, will help people understand when you then ask them not to use their cigarette lighters to light their own candles, but to wait for the Paschal light.

Very simple things often get overlooked. For example, invite people to turn around to look at the fire, or to go outside if it is outside, as otherwise they may miss that whole part of the ceremony. In general people do not feel free to move in church, not even to turn around, so it is important to invite them to do so. Also, when offering such an invitation, use a phrase like 'Let us now ...' rather than giving instructions.

In some parishes there is a 'commentator' who will describe the unfamiliar parts of the liturgy, explain any symbolic significance and invite participation where appropriate. The key is to be succinct.

Many aspects of the liturgy benefit from rehearsal, especially any processions and the story telling.

Tonight's ceremony is made up of four distinct celebrations:

> Festival of Light
> Festival of the Story
> Festival of Water and
> Festival of the Eucharist.

Suggestions for celebrating the Eucharist will be made in Part III.

Festival of Light

The fire should be big, it should be outside, and everyone should be gathered around it.

If this is not possible, think of ways you can gather as many people around a smaller fire at the back of the church. Maybe invite all the children or young people to come to the back of the church – they could then be the ones to spread the light through the congregation.

Whether your fire is inside or outside, have a fire-extinguisher at hand.

The church should be in total darkness (the presider can use a little torch if they need to read the text), and the light should spread from the Paschal Candle.

If you are gathering outside, have people go round with baskets outside, giving a candle to each person as they arrive. If people are gathering inside, leave the candles on the pews/seats (with cardboard protectors too if you can) before people come in or have the greeters at the door give them out to each person as they come in .

The whole congregation could gather around a fire lit outside the church and then process around the church (and even part of the neighbourhood), culminating in a procession of light into the church itself.

Preserve the sense of wonder at the arrival of the light by leaving the church lit only by the candles for as long as posssible – right up to the Easter proclamation at least, or even to the Liturgy of the Word.

Festival of the Story

The readings are stories, so try to think of ways you can *tell* them rather than *read* them.

Certain of the stories could be acted out (eg. Abraham's sacrifice of Isaac, or use hoops with streamers and have people pass through them as they pass through the red sea).

You could create a 'river' of creation with a long blue cloth or net stretching from the aisle up to the altar and as the story of creation is told, place all kind of things in it. (These could later be incorporated into the presentation of gifts).

Use these stories as an opportunity to involve a cross-section of the community – eg. the children could do the creation story, the young people or drama group could act out the sacrifice, an older person who is gifted as a storyteller could tell one of the stories in his or her own style, parents could organise a slide display with their own photos to accompany one of the stories.

You could tell one of the stories in the Seder format (particularly the Exodus story). The Seder is the Jewish Passover meal, the ancestor of the Christian Easter rituals. During the Seder, all the younger participants are encouraged to ask questions and the older ones have to answer them as enthusiastically and thoroughly as possible. So a group could gather in the sanctuary, and the youngest ask, 'What is it we celebrate this night that is different to all other nights?' and the older storytellers reply, re-telling the scripture in their own words. Involve as many people as possible, and make sure they can all be heard (moveable microphones are helpful).

Use music/sound, slide displays, mime or dance in sup-
port of the readings to help the story live in the senses of
the listener.

The Psalms should be sung, not said. Yes, all of them!

The Alleluia should be an almighty Alleluia tonight. Sing
it out, and process the Gospel Book, decorated if you like,
for all to see.

Festival of Water/Baptism
Water should be much in evidence – people should be able
to see it, touch it and especially hear it.

Make the baptismal font visible, either at the door where
people come in, or up by the altar. It should really be visible all the time, as a constant reminder of our baptism, and
the responsibility that brings.

You can buy a water pump for about £30, and make a
'fountain' as a font – this will give a lovely gurgling sound
behind the whole celebration.

Or build a 'well' – stones and moss around a large bowl.

Or play a tape recording of a babbling brook.

Or else have a large bowl of water with a big jug in it at the
entrance, or in the central aisle, or on the altar – it is a good
visual aid, but people should also be encouraged to dip
their hands in it, and to pour water from jug to basin as
they pass it.

In small churches, everyone should gather around the

well/font. In large churches, the water should be processed up the aisle, with lots of people (at least twenty!) involved.

Explain what the significance of water would have been in
Jesus' culture: for us it is abundant and often the subject of
our complaints, for them it was scarce and precious.

Perhaps instead of blessing the whole congregation, people
could be blessed individually. If they are gathered round a
water source/font they could bless themselves, or bowls
of water could be passed around and people bless one another (passed along the pews like a collection plate).

At the renewal of baptismal promises, the congregation
could say more than just, 'We do' to each of the priest's
questions. One simple idea is to split the congregation in
two and let each side turn and face the other. Each half
then asks the other the questions in turn (this way everyone actually says the words of the profession of faith and
has to look at their faith community directly).

Easter Vigil: Further Suggestions

Celia Hayes

The *Festival of Light* is concerned with
• Exploring the darkness.
• Remembering, experiencing, and sharing in the darkness which the chosen people experienced before Christ's birth.
• Acknowledging our own sinfulness or inner darkness and, in so doing, celebrating our salvation.

The *Festival* aims to
• Symbolically present the journey from darkness to light.
• Focus upon our individual and community journey towards light.
• Emphasise that each of us experiences inner darkness in our personal journey with Christ and in the community.
• Celebrate the resurrection of Christ.

Creatively in the *Festival of Light* we aim to
• Touch the hearts and senses of those gathered so as to lead them into a deeper, more meaningful reality.
• Create moments of wonder that words cannot explain or fully describe.
• Evoke the senses.
• Infuse the congregation with a sense of God.
• Facilitate the Spirit.
• Create and hold something magical.
• Dispel the darkness.

How is this done? *Some practical suggestions:*
• Dim the lights inside the church and process in.
• Process from the source (wherever it may be) to various positions around the congregation.
• Roll back a stone from the tomb to reveal the light. (A tomb is easy to build. Use cheap materials and a little creativity.)
• Place the Easter Fire in a focal position in the church.
• Hold the silence and semi-darkness for long enough for the Spirit to work.

Maintaining a meaningful silence with a large congregation in semi-darkness can be a very powerful, prayerful experience. All too often, words inadequately express what this part of the ceremony evokes in the hearts and senses of the gathered community. Occasionally the ambience and atmosphere of this particular ceremony can generate 'something so beautiful it can't be expressed in words, and makes your heart ache because of it.' So, dare to hold the silence and use it to facilitate the work of the Spirit. Allow it to create and nourish wonder in this unique ceremony.

The *Festival of Story* is concerned with
• Arousing and holding the attention of the gathered community.
• Telling a story or passing on information.
• Holding the listeners' interest.
• Exciting and amusing them.
• Appealing to their emotions.

How is this done? *Some practical suggestions:*
• Tell the story. There is simply no substitute for good storytelling. When and where possible, seek out, find and

encourage a good storyteller to participate in the liturgy. The story can take several forms. It can be presented in dialogue or narrative form. It may be told by a senior family member to an interested junior, as happens in the Jewish Seder. It may occur as a news item, a poem, song or short play.

• Mime the story. Remember that mime requires a lot of preparation and expertise.

• Act the story out. Invite local talent and school groups to get involved. A project such as this can be rotated within the various community groups from year to year.

• Add background music to the telling of the story. This can enhance the atmosphere or create a particular mood. This idea is simple and can be quite effective, reflective and evocative.

• Present the story as a meditation.

• Use slides accompanied by a tape. An unusual yet beautifully captive from of storytelling. Ensure that the sound is clear and the overhead visible.

• Read the story. Sounds familiar? It is ... so do it well!

• Sing it. The music of Andrew Lloyd Weber, Michael Card or John Michael Talbot could be useful here.

• Present the story in picture form, or a collage. Again the local schools can be of help here.

Who might help?

• Encourage local parish groups to lend a hand with the preparation, planning and implementation of ideas. These can include drama societies, choirs, art groups, musicians, schools, storytellers, etc.

• Work with youth clubs, Foroige and Gaisce participants.

• Be courageous enough to use the natural talent available in your locality. You may be pleasantly surprised at what you discover. Good luck!

Easter Vigil: Suggested Music

Francis McMyler

Lumen Christi:
Deo Gratias (3) (*Roman Missal*)
After the third Deo Gratias, all sing
He is Lord (*Hymns Old & New 206*)

During the Exultet:
Response interspersed:
Rejoice to greet the Risen Lord

At the end of the Exultet:
Amen (*Roman Missal*)

At the end of the Exodus reading:
I will sing to the Lord (*Responsorial Psalms for Sundays and
Major Feasts, Irish Church Music Association*)

Alleluia:
Praise to you Lord Jesus Christ
King of endless glory
(*Fintan O'Carroll*)

Blessing of Water:
Alleluia – interspersed
Water of Life (*Hosanna 220*)

Holy, holy:

Mass of the Immaculate Conception

(*Fintan O'Carroll*)

Acclamation:

Dying you destroyed our death

(*Jean Paul Lécot, Mass of Our Lady of Lourdes*)

Amen:

(*Jean Paul Lécot, Mass of Our Lady of Lourdes*)

Holy Communion

We have been told (*Hosanna 119*)

Ubi Caritas (*Music from Taizé, Bk 1*)

Recessional:

Thine be the glory (*Handel, Judas Maccabaeus*)

or

Jesus Christ is risen today (*Veritas Hymnal 102*)

PART II

Good Friday

Good Friday
– a theological note

Enda Lyons

The last three days of Holy Week should not be seen as celebrating three separate events. They mark, rather, three moments in a great single event – the divine event of Jesus being 'brought out' by the Father from this life, through death, to eternal life – they celebrate Jesus' death and resurrection and, in this, *our* exodus too. The Easter Vigil, then, should not be seen as just coming *after* Good Friday. It celebrates the final outcome of that event and marks God's final approval and acceptance of it. Good Friday is the gateway to the resurrection and not just a prelude to it. Its significance can really be understood only in the light of the resurrection.

1. What we celebrate on Good Friday

Our first question regarding the Good Friday liturgy concerns the meaning of the event into which this celebration seeks to draw us. Throughout the centuries this event has been, and continues to be today, experienced by Christians as having literally and immeasurable depth of meaning. Only a few aspects of this meaning can be touched on here.

1. The Death of Jesus
The first and most obvious event celebrated on Good Friday is the death of Jesus. Regarding this there are a few

points in particular which we might need to remember today.

i) There is its *awfulness.* Today we rightly try to make our crucifixes more artistic and beautiful. This, however, ought not to mean sweetening or over-sanitising the cross. The death of Jesus was a most terrible one. It was the result of his being nailed to a cross and left hanging from these nails until, his physical endurance utterly exhausted, he finally expired.

ii) There is the *cause* of Jesus' death, about which there can be much confusion in Christians' minds. In this connection we should carefully avoid such crude ideas as that which sees Jesus used by God as a scape-goat for human sin, and his death imposed – unjustly – by God as the price of the forgiveness of the sins of others. The Christian conviction that Jesus died on our behalf may not be interpreted as meaning that God punished him unjustly in our stead. God cannot be thought of as *wanting* or *wishing* the terrible death of Jesus any more than God can be thought of as wanting or wishing any other evil act. Jesus was, we are reminded in the gospel stories of his baptism and transfiguration, the beloved Son in whom the Father delighted and was 'well pleased' (eg. Mk 1:11, 9:7). His death, it needs to be clearly understood, was fully the result of human resistance to and rejection of what he stood for.

Nor ought we think of Jesus as purposely looking for his death, seeking it out with some sort of death-wish. In the agony scene we read of him praying that, if possible, he should be spared it:

    … a sudden fear came over him, and great distress.
    And he said to them, 'My soul is sorrowful to the point

of death. And going on a little further he threw himself on the ground and prayed that, if it were possible, this hour might pass him by (Mk 14:33-36).

The death on the cross was one which Jesus *accepted* rather than positively sought out. Jesus willingly accepted it as the consequence and price of remaining faithful to what he had all his life, lived for – loving service of people and of God.

iii) There is also the fact that what we celebrate today is not just the death of Jesus but his *dying*. For death and dying are not always the same thing. Death can be seen as just a physical event, the termination of life, a perishing. Death in that sense comes to all living things, plants, animals and humans alike. For a human being, however, death is not just something which is imposed and which has simply to be endured. In the case of humans death can be foreseen as the inevitable ending of life. For a human, then, death, can and, indeed, ought to be voluntarily accepted and entered into. Paradoxically it can be, and ought to be, 'lived'. When it is 'lived' it becomes a *human* act, our final human act. It also becomes our most significant human act for it is the final handing back of our life, in faith and trust, to the Source from which it came as a gift. On Good Friday Jesus was not just despoiled of his life by others. When faced with the inevitability of his death he willingly gave over his life, for the sake of those in whose service he had spent it, to the One from whom he had received it:

Father, into your hands I commit my spirit (Lk 23:46).

Since throughout his life Jesus had continually been hand-ing over his life for others, this final act of giving it up was a consummation of his whole life. It was, to echo a phrase of Karl Rahner, the death of his dying. It was because of this *dying*, rather than just this death that God raised Jesus up:

> ... he was humbler yet,
> even to accepting death,
> death on a cross.
> But God raised him high
> and gave him the name
> which is above all other names ...
> (Phil 2:9)

2. *The Power of Evil*

On Good Friday we are drawn into a second experience, that of the power of evil, of the awful potential of human evil. Jesus, it needs hardly be said, was a good man. During his life he stood for nothing except good and against nothing except what is destructive of human living. His life's work was to establish in the world 'the reign of God', that is, to set up

> ... a kingdom of *truth* and *life*,
> a kingdom of *holiness* and *grace*,
> a kingdom of *justice, love,* and *peace*
> (Preface of the Mass of Christ the King).

His death was the result of the rejection of that goodness. Prominent among those who rejected it were those in positions of power both secular and religious. The following passage written by the Lutheran theologian Dietrich Bonhoeffer, who himself was executed in the cause of right, reminds us that the power of evil has not yet disappeared from our world. It also reminds us of how Jesus responded to it:

> Jesus, the man alone
> abandoned by his disciples and friends

rejected by the religious authorities as too dangerous
making life uncomfortable by his questions
challenging long established customs
inviting people to relate to God directly
rejected by the political authorities
as a disturber of the peace
upsetting the equilibrium of Roman-Jewish relations
a harmless simple man
yet subverting the 'peace' of society
rejected by his fellow citizens as a failure
for not fulfilling their political expectations
not satisfying their search for
higher economic standards
the man alone–
this man
whose bones are crushed by nails
whose body is held taut by its position
pinioned on wood
this man
asks his Father to forgive them.

Jesus, the man alone –
In the passion Jesus is a rejected Messiah... To die on
the Cross meant to die despised and rejected by men.
(quoted by Alan Falconer in *A Man Alone,* Dublin,
Columba Press, 1994, p 26).

3. *The Mystery of God's Love*

On Good Friday we celebrate too the incomprehensible
mystery of God identifying with us in our suffering. Jesus,
we celebrated at Christmas, is *Emmanuel,* God-with-us.
Jesus crucified on the cross is still *Emmanuel,* but now he is
God-with-us in our suffering, in this most degrading suffering. For Jesus' death was the degrading death of a crim-

inal – death as a result of a death penalty inflicted with the
full approval of the civil and religious authorities of his
country. In the death of Jesus we see God, in Jesus, bearing
the full brunt of human evil, absorbing it into the divine
forgiveness and, so, rendering it in an ultimate sense pow-
erless – in a word, redeeming it.

2. The Rituals Recommended

The rituals for drawing us into the Good Friday event
which are prescribed in the Missal are four:

1. Atmosphere/environment/setting

The importance of the recommendations regarding the atmosphere and environment and setting for this liturgy
could easily be overlooked. They ought not be because
they set the tone for the celebration and have great potential for drawing us into it.

The atmosphere, it is recommended, should be quiet,
solemn and bare – a bare altar, an open tabernacle door, no
flowers and, to begin with at least, no lighted candles.

The ministers enter in silence. They prostrate themselves
on the ground. Before any word is uttered, all pray in silence for a period. When eventually the silence is broken it
is broken only with a simple key-note prayer.

If the resurrection of Jesus is a glorious and joyful moment,
the dying which preceded it and made it possible is a moment of aloneness, isolation and pain. It is devoid of all
glamour.

2. Word

In tune with the whole atmosphere, the liturgy moves
without fanfare or fuss into the liturgy of the Word.
During this, three verbal pictures are drawn, each taking
us into the Good Friday event and evoking from us a response in psalm or in prayer.

The description of *The Suffering Servant* from Isaiah chapter 52 presents a stark picture of a suffering one. It is familiar to Christians because of its frequent application to
Christ:

'... the crowds were appalled on seeing him – so disfig-
ured did he look ...'

'... without beauty, without majesty, no looks to attract
our eyes ...'

'... a man of sorrows and familiar with suffering...'

'... a man to make people screen their faces ...'

'... he was despised and we took no account of him ...'

'... like a lamb ... led to the slaughter, like a sheep ...
dumb before his shearers, never opening his mouth ...'

– a beautiful, even poetic, reading this.

The reading from the *Letter to the Hebrews* touches on the
meaning which the Passion has for us. Jesus, and in him
God, we are reminded, has experienced not only our physical suffering, but also our moments of mental anguish –
our 'silent tears':

During his life on earth, Jesus offered up prayer and entreaty aloud and in silent tears ... Although he was a
Son, he learned to obey through suffering ... (Heb 5:7, 9).

Perhaps, in the end, it is only this thought which will help
us to face, even though still puzzled and uncomfortable,
the mystery of the suffering and the evil which is all
around us and, perhaps more significantly, within us.

In the *Acclamation* we proclaim, in the words of the Letter to the Phillippians, Jesus' willing acceptance of his death – his dying.

The Liturgy of the Word reaches its climax in an account of *The Passion*. Today the account proclaimed is that according to John. Like John's gospel as a whole this account differs considerably in its purpose, and in its presentation of Jesus, from that of the other gospels. John's gospel was written with the definite purpose of emphasising that Jesus from birth to death was *the Eternal Word made flesh*, the one who had come from God and was to return to God. The Jesus portrayed in John's account of the Passion is, accordingly, serene, majestic and in perfect control. This is particularly evident throughout his great encounter with Pilate. The portrayal of Jesus in John's Passion is not meant to distract us from the reality of Jesus' suffering, from the picture of that 'man of sorrows familiar with suffering ..., a man to make people screen their faces', offering up during his life 'prayer and entreaty aloud and in silent tears'. It does, however, provide a necessary balance in our picture of the suffering Jesus. Terrible and degrading though his pain was, Jesus was always, in a profound way, serenely in control. While he suffered dreadfully on the Cross he also reigned from it.

As a response to this passion narrative there follow *General Intercessions*. These are ten prayers each having the same structure:

> i) an invitation to all present to pray for a particular intention,
> ii) a pause to give time for that prayer,
> iii) a formal gathering together, a 'collecting', of the silent prayers (a *Collect*),
> iv) an assenting *Amen*.

The great characteristic of these prayers is their *universality*. There is a prayer, for example, for those preparing for baptism and one for those who do not believe in God; there is a prayer for the pope and a prayer for civic leaders, one for all Christians and one for all Jews. In the end there is a prayer for all those in special need– for the sick and the dying, for travellers, for those deprived of their freedom, for the victims of world-hunger and disease, for those who have lost heart and for all 'who cry out to God in any trouble'. These prayers embrace the whole world as Christians believe Jesus did with his arms outstretched on the cross. They seem to flow from the Passion story and make their way around the world as, in John's gospel, blood and water from the side of Christ on the cross (Jn 19:34).

3. The Cross

As might be expected the cross is the great symbol in this liturgy. Much is made of its power to draw us into the Good Friday event.

There is its *solemn introduction* to the assembled congregation while it is being publicly unveiled or carried in procession through the church. It is accompanied by lighted candles – their first appearance in this liturgy.

There is, during this, the threefold *communal veneration* of the cross – the threefold invitation to all to venerate, together, the cross, and the threefold communal response to this invitation:

> *Invitation:* This is the wood on the cross, on which hung the Saviour of the world.
>
> *Response:* Come, let us worship (after which response all kneel).

There is the *individual veneration* when our sense of *touch* is engaged in order to draw us more deeply into the cross of Jesus. During this period songs and psalms are sung – the power of music too is employed to engage us in what is happening.

4. Holy Communion

There is no Mass in this major liturgy which, especially in a Roman Catholic context, is a most powerful ritual in itself.

The liturgy comes to an end in *The Holy Communion Service*. Here an opportunity of *receiving* the sacrament of the body and blood of the Crucified and Risen Lord is offered. If the purpose of ritual is to draw us into an event by engaging the *whole* person, this is a most powerful ritual moment.

After the Communion Service, the rubric is, 'All depart in silence'. The great Liturgy of Good Friday fittingly ends as it began – in silence.

Good Friday: A Living Liturgy

Siobhán Garrigan

General Guidelines

The Triduum – the three services that make up the celebration of Easter – is really one event. So the Good Friday celebration of the Lord's Passion is part of the wider celebration of his resurrection.

It is important to remember this, because without this understanding it would be easy to interpret Friday's liturgy as a sort of funeral. It is not. It is about the fact that Jesus' resurrection is not separated from his death – through the cross joy was brought to the world.

Hence ministers wear red (and encourage your readers – they are ministers of the Word – to wear a colour other than black).

Try to use a plain cross instead of a crucifix.

Think about how it is displayed as part of your general thoughts about the space that people enter.

You might also like to think about other potential symbols you could display in the entrance or in the sanctuary which will enable people to focus on the meaning of the ritual space (crown of thorns, an unlighted candle, bogoak sculpture, a photograph of a modern-day calvary). Some churches clear everything except the pulpit from the altar and so engage people in the space through absence, not presence.

It may be helpful to have quiet reflective music playing as people enter.

The atmosphere should be quiet, solemn and prayerful. But not miserable.

One of the dangers facing the Good Friday celebration is that it may become too wordy. So really try to use symbols prominently and to use music (both solos and congregational singing, as well as reflective pieces) plentifully.

It is not appropriate to have the sacrament of penance/reconciliation on this day, communally or individually. Lent is the time for penitence in preparation for the Triduum.

This celebration has a long and interesting history. You may like to read about it in one of the following books:
Gabe Huck: *The Three Days*
Kenneth Stevenson: *Jerusalem Revisited: the Liturgical Meaning of Holy Week*
Brian Magee CM: *In the Light of Christ*

The entrance should be very simple (not a grand procession) and the presider and two others should prostrate while the congregation adopts a position of prayer (traditionally kneeling). Don't forget to tell the congregation that this is what is to be expected.

The ceremony has four main movements:

Liturgy of the Word
Prayers of the Faithful (technically part of the Liturgy of
the Word)
Veneration of the Cross
Communion Rite.

Liturgy of the Word
First Reading is from Isaiah: see Appendix A for a participatory version.

The Psalm is 'into your hands …'
• It should be sung
• It could be led by a youth group (or other group)
• It could be accompanied by a procession of all the things
we put into God's hands.

The gospel is the passion according to John
• People should be invited to sit down
• The reading should be divided into at least three voices
• Many people do not like that their part is to say 'Crucify
him'. You could have a group do these parts, or …
• You could incorporate a simple liturgical gesture, eg.
while a single reader says 'Crucify him!' each person in the
congregation raises both arms toward the cross, or falls on
one knee
• You could sing 'Were you there when they crucified my
God' at certain points
• The reading could be accompanied by a slide display
• It could be acted out (all of it, or part of it) – again, telling
rather than reading the story.

If there is to be any sermon (which is not usual), it should
be very short so that the symbolic quality of the ceremony
is primary.

Prayers of the Faithful
There are usually ten. The aim is to maintain an atmosphere of prayer and so avoid boredom or monotony.

Technically one is supposed to kneel or stand. In practice a prayerful mood may be more accessible if one is seated.

Vary the voices (and involve a cross section of the community, not just a single reader) of those reading the intention. The priest then reads just the actual prayer after the pause.

Maintain a good pause to enable individual interpretation. Most pauses should be silent, but one or two could be enhanced by musical or visual reflection.

Sing a refrain, a 'Hear our Prayer' as a response to each prayer (this enables all to assent in a fuller way).

Have some symbolic visual representation for each of the prayers spread, like Stations of the Cross, around the sides of the building. The readers and presider then go to each 'Station' as the prayer for that concern is raised. (This could be done as a collage of newspaper clippings, a patchwork, a painting, a child's drawing, a scuplture or an object – and could be co-ordinated by children, youth, ICA, SVP, etc).

Veneration of the Cross
There should be only one cross, ideally.

Regarding individual veneration, the important thing is that everyone can venerate the cross in a meaningful way: they should not feel rushed. So whatever way you organise it, make sure people feel they have the time they need.

People can venerate the cross in a variety of ways: by a kiss, by a genuflection, a bow, or a simple touch. They should be encouraged to do what they feel most comfortable doing.

People could venerate the cross in their own time after the ceremony if they so wish.

There are various other ways of deepening our experience of the cross. For example, set a large, broad, plain cross in the church on Palm Sunday and from that day on, encourage people to bring in clippings from the papers of suffering at home and in the wider world. By Good Friday, the cross will be covered, and reading the articles and offering a prayer in front of the cross becomes a form of veneration.

Alternatively, in some parishes, there is a polystyrene cross covered with plain material and each person places a nail in it when they venerate it. This can be extended by each person removing another's nail when they leave the church after their watch is complete.

It has become a common enough practice now not to sing the reproaches (because they are seen as funereal and therefore at odds with the wider theology of the Triduum), but it is important to sing something while those who wish to venerate the cross during the body of the liturgy do so.

Sing right up until the communion service is ready to begin.

Communion Rite

This is not strictly necessary, but most places still do it. The altar should be stripped as soon as the sacrament is taken to repose.

Emphasis should remain on the central part of this liturgy (ie. the passion and cross), not on the communion rite or the removal of the elements, so this part should be brief and simple.

Dismissal should be in silence. Total silence (no music).

Good Friday: Further Suggestions

Celia Hayes

Some suggestions

• The Passion reading may be done in dialogue form, during which the cross can be slowly revealed, stage by stage.

• The Good Friday Cross is a large cross, onto which newspaper cuttings depicting contemporary human suffering may be stuck each day during Lent. This cross can be placed in the front porch of the church and added to daily by worshippers. By Good Friday, this cross may be moved to the altar, if so desired.

• The General Intercessions may be said around the Good Friday Cross.

• Veneration: perhaps a moment of prayer before the Good Friday Cross ... lay one's own suffering there at/with it.

• Splinter Cross: This is a cross made from splints by the congregation. The following is an example of how it might be used:

'Today is a day when we are reminded about Christ's suffering in a special way. As we commemorate his passion, we recognise our own suffering here in our own community. It can take many forms:

> death/bereavement
> unemployment
> illness
> anxiety/worry
> broken relationships
> addiction
> separation from God …

We want to acknowledge the existence of suffering and show that we are willing to carry a Splinter Cross in our lives. We invite each member of the congregation to take a piece of wood from the basket of splints provided (as you leave, or at a different stage of the liturgy) and to place it within the outline of a large cross on the floor, (which will have been prepared earlier). Together as a community, we will create a cross with our splints. We will acknowledge each others' sufferings and thank God for the gift of his Son Jesus and thank Jesus for the gift of his suffering, death and resurrection.

Good Friday: Suggested Music

Francis McMyler

Responsorial Psalm:
Father, I put my life
my life in your hands
(*Marty Haugen, Psalms for the Church Year, Vol 1*)

Prayers of Intercession:
Hear our prayer (*Earnest Sands, OCP ed 7206*)
or
Let us pray to the Lord (Byzantine)
(*Mass of Our Lady of Lourdes*)
or
O Lord, hear us we pray,
O Lord, give us your love
(*Lucien Deiss, More Biblical Hymns & Psalms*)

Veneration of the Cross:
This is the wood of the cross (*Roman Missal*)

During the veneration:
Jesus remember me (Taizé) (*Hosanna 196*)
Confitemini Domino (*Music from Taizé, Vol 2*)
Were you there? (*Gather, 171*)
Salvator Mundi salva nos (*Music from Taizé, Vol 1*)

Procession from the Altar of Repose:
Praise to the Holiest (*R. P. Terry, Veritas Hymnal 82*)

Holy Communion:
Ubi Caritas (*Music from Taizé, Vol 1*)
Soul of my Saviour (*Veritas Hymnal 32*)

PART III

Holy Thursday

Holy Thursday:

Deepening our Appreciation for Eucharist

Eugene Duffy

The liturgy of Holy Thursday evening is above all a com-memoration of the Last Supper and the institution of the Eucharist by Jesus. It is an evening celebration. The signifi-cance of the time is that for the Jewish people, to whom we are closely linked by faith and traditions, the day begins with sundown. Therefore, the timing of the liturgy suggests that there is an intimate connection between what is hap-pening on this evening and what will happen on Good Friday. In fact the antiphon makes the connection between this evening's liturgy and the liturgies of the following two days: 'We should glory in the cross of Our Lord Jesus Christ, for he is our salvation, our life and our resurrection; through him we are saved and made free.' These words point to the full scope of the paschal mystery which is about to be cele-brated and to the joy that Christians find in realising that they and all peoples have been liberated from the powers of evil, sin and death. This liberation has been effected by the loving service of Jesus, through his life, death and resurrec-tion, and is now commemorated and celebrated in the Eucharist.

On this evening the readings, the prayers, and the rituals draw us into the stories and events that lay the foundations for our celebration of the Eucharist. The focus is sharp: the Passover Meal, St Paul's account of the Last Supper and a telling detail from the table, provided by St John, elucidating the implications of sharing in the eucharistic celebration – even to the humble service of washing feet. This concentrated focus on the events of Holy Thursday serve to remind us of what it is that is happening each time we gather for Eucharist. Therefore, in this chapter attention will be drawn to a contemporary understanding of Eucharist that will provide a background not only for those planning the liturgy of Holy Thursday but for all those who wish to deepen their appreciation of this central Christian sacrament. Indeed, contemporary eucharistic theology focuses on the liturgical action as a whole, stressing equally that it is a sacred banquet, a memorial and a sacrifice offered by the gathered assembly, not just by the presiding priest.

The Trinity and the Eucharist

The Christian belief in a triune God has to condition all of our theological endeavours. A useful way to introduce ourselves to the central mystery of the triune God is to look at the Rublev Hospitality Icon. Through figures, colours and symbols the artist conveys more eloquently than any words an appreciation of the life of the Trinity and the unfolding plan of God, the great mystery about which St Paul speaks in the letter to the Ephesians (1:13-14).

The three persons are seated around the table, bonded together in a fellowship of love. They are tuned outward towards the world with an attentive gaze, ready to welcome their guests around their table. This is a liturgy of hospitality, joy and blessedness, a liturgy which will only be fully realised when all their guests share in their banquet.

Banquet of life for all

The Son goes out from that table and in the person of Jesus

of Nazareth makes known to the human family what is on offer for them. He issues the invitation to join that table-fellowship in the most personal way possible. The invitation is not presented as something in a distant future but as something which can begin to be experienced in the present. Jesus in his own life and ministry gives a concrete expression of what that table-fellowship really means.

Jesus embodied the compassion of God in a great variety of ways, both in word and in action. His preaching of the reign of God heralded a new Exodus, the ending of a long exile and the ultimate triumph over the powers of evil. The vision of the new future was spelled out in parables which spoke of profound reconciliation, prodigal love and un-bounded joy. This new future was embodied concretely in the healing ministry of Jesus but above all in the meals which he shared with those whom he encountered.

Jesus cut through the prejudices which religious people had erected in a way which is difficult for us to imagine. He accepted around his table everybody, no matter what their background or social standing. He accepted people as they were, as fellow human beings, so that they felt for-given, reconciled and part of the wider community (see Luke 14:15-24). He enabled people to feel genuinely human again, with their dignity restored. He gave them fresh in-sight into their unique worth and value before God and one another.

The sheer prodigality of God's love is also evident in the context of other meals which Jesus enriched by providing food and drink for the participants. When the drink ran out at Cana he provided a generous draft of good fresh wine. He did not want to see the enjoyment of the occasion in any way diminished. Similarly, we find him, again in John's gospel, providing an abundance of food for those who are tired and hungry at the end of a long day on the hillside.

As well as responding to the immediate needs of the people, Jesus was giving them a foretaste of the messianic banquet. The abundance of Jesus' provisions was merely an anticipation of that great banquet when:

Yahweh Sabaoth will prepare for all peoples
a banquet of rich food,
a banquet of fine wines,
of food rich and juicy,
of fine strained wines (Is 25:6).

None of the implications of the table-fellowship of Jesus, neither its generosity nor its inclusiveness nor its eschatological significance, were lost on those who witnessed it. All of these fuelled the desire of his opponents to be rid of him. Nevertheless, Jesus was not deterred by this opposition. Rather was he determined to remain resolutely committed to the plan of God, the advancement of God's reign on earth.

A consideration of the meals of Jesus provides an important context both for the Last Supper itself and for Eucharist which is, from a liturgical perspective, a ritual meal. His table-fellowship is still a challenge to us as we gather to celebrate Eucharist, raising questions about our attention to human dignity, prejudice and unconditional love.

The Last Supper
When he finally went up to Jerusalem for the Passover of

that year Jesus must have been acutely aware of the
mounting opposition to him and his message. He must
also have been aware that the Passover celebration was a
time of tension in the city and that anyone who was re-
garded as a threat to the peace and stability of the nation
was likely to be executed.

These two factors provide the critical background against
which we begin to understand the Last Supper. These real-
ities provide an important horizon of understanding for
the disciples and for us of a later generation. They lead us
into an exploration of a key idea of eucharistic understanding, namely, that of memorial.

The Eucharist as memorial

We cannot be sure that the Last Supper itself was in fact a
Passover meal but what we can say is that it was celebrated
in the context of the Passover. Central to the Passover celebration was the concept of memorial. The memorial was
more than a remembering of the past events of the Exodus.
Through ritual action and a familiar accompanying narrative, the people were enabled to share in the original
experience of their ancestors who journeyed from the slavery of Egypt to the freedom of the promised land. The
food, the dress, the posture and people present were all
meant to conspire in evoking something of that original
experience which effected their liberation and their consti-
tution as the people of God.

The Jewish memorial was meant to act as a ritual through
which the people thanked God for what God had done in
the past and on the basis of this goodness, this steadfast
love, they pleaded with God to continue showing that
kind of love into the future. Memorial also reminded God

of the divine favour shown them and made a claim on the basis of past experience that God would bring to fulfilment the work already begun.

Perhaps one of the clearest instances of memorial in the Old Testament is that which occurs in the book of Nehemiah (Ch 9). The context is that the people have returned from their exile in Babylon. They are in Jerusalem, a city which has been destroyed. Their leaders have no idea how they are going to rebuild what has been destroyed nor how their future will look. Instead of wallowing in self-pity and despair they gathered the people and in the presence of the assembly begin to recapitulate the long catalogue of favourable deeds which their God has worked on their behalf. Despite the vicissitudes of history and the infidelities of the people, God always remained constant in goodness and mercy. Reflection on the past gives them every confidence to believe and hope that this same God will continue to show favour into the future and will provide for the good of all the people.

This background is important, too, for an understanding of what Jesus was doing in the words and actions of the Last Supper. His own situation of desolation was significant. He had given his life entirely to preaching the immediacy of God's reign and giving people concrete experiences of its impact on their lives. Now, as he faced the prospect of violent death, it may seem as if the forces of evil and those who could not accept him were about to be vindicated. It is against such a devastating vista that he summoned his disciples to gather with him around the table and to share this last meal of fellowship with him.

Given the Passover context, it is entirely likely that Jesus

recapitulated and proclaimed the steadfast love of God as
this had been made manifest in the history of the people of
Israel and also in his own life. He must have renewed his
own sense of gratitude to God for what God had done in
him and reaffirmed his own commitment to face death
rather than retract anything he had previously said or
done in God's name. Although the only horizon which lay
ahead of him was death, he seemed determined to face it
with a certain confidence that, even in this hour of darkness and human uncertainty, God would act and bring a
new future out of an otherwise destructive event. Jesus
can then be understood to have faced death with confidence in God's abiding love but without knowing the
shape which God's future might take. His confidence was
such that he could say to his disciples that even his own
body would be taken up into the shaping of that future.
Thus he could give over his body to them and to the Father
in a confident surrender of loving service. So his own body
was to be part of the future which God was now shaping.
It is only in the light of the resurrection that the full implications of what Jesus said and did at the Last Supper could
be fully appreciated. Only resurrection light can elucidate
the full significance of Jesus' command to 'do this as a
memorial of me'.

Thanksgiving
The Eucharist itself is then understood as a memorial in
the light of this Jewish faith and liturgical context in which
it was first celebrated. The memorial is an act both of gratitude and of supplication. Thanksgiving was always
stressed as an important dimension of the eucharistic action. In addition to the reasons for which the Jewish people might thank God, the disciples of Jesus had further
reasons for expressing their gratitude. They now thanked

God for what was done for them in the life, death and resurrection of Jesus. Furthermore, on the basis of this divine
favour they pleaded God with renewed confidence, asking that what was begun in the Christ event would be
brought to completion for all of them. Thus it is that all the
eucharistic prayers are directed to the Father.

The memorial of the Eucharist is much more than a subjec-
tive remembrance. In the Eucharist the past event of the
death and resurrection of Christ is sacramentally present
through the liturgical action. Not only is the saving event
of the past sacramentally present but the very person of
the victim is present as a resurrected and transfigured
body. Here we cross over into the realm of faith percep-
tion. The faith conviction of the church is that in the eucharistic action the risen Christ is present to the community
in a uniquely personal way, albeit under the appearances
of bead and wine.

The Eucharist as sacrifice

Our notion of sacrifice needs a little retrieval. Sacrifice is a
way in which the offerer expresses the desire to be in
union with God and it involves making a significant gesture which demonstrates that deep self-commitment. In
the Old Testament a person took an animal or food or
something else which was precious and offered it to God
as a sign of his or her desire to be in real communion with
God and to enjoy God's favour.

The offering was, however, only one side of the sacrifice. It
had to be accepted by God in order for the transaction to
be complete. The acceptance was signified by the sacrifice
being consumed by fire (2 Chr 7:1-3); by the smoke of the
burnt offering rising up to God (Lev 9:22-24; Exod 19:18);

more commonly by the word spoken by the presiding priest (2 Sam 24:23; Ezek 43:27). The acceptance of the sacrifice is essential to its very nature because without acceptance there is no sacrifice.

Three of the main sacrifices of the Old Testament were:

i) the original Passover sacrifice where the blood of the lamb was sprinkled on the door-posts of the Hebrew tents to ensure the protection of the people when the angel of destruction passed by during the night (Exod 12);

ii) the Covenant sacrifice offered during the Exodus when Moses sprinkled the blood of the bull on the altar and on the people, sealing their desire to be forever in communion with God and with one another (Exod 24:8);

iii) the Day of Atonement when sacrifices were offered as sin offerings, for the remission of the sins of the people (Lev 16).

In all of these sacrifices blood played an important role. Blood was sacred because it was the symbol of life and life belonged exclusively to God. Therefore in the pouring out of blood the person offering was pouring out his or her own self before God, signifying the desire for communion of life with God. These ideas underlie our understanding of the Eucharist as a sacrifice.

The New Testament clearly understands the death of Jesus as a sacrificial offering. The offering of Jesus is very different from any of the offerings of the Old Testament. In all previous sacrifices the offerer used an animal or something else precious to signify the desire to be in communion of life with God. In the case of Jesus he offers himself totally, shedding his own blood as an expression of his desire to please God and to carry out the mission to which he had been called. His death was freely chosen as a way of demonstrating his total commitment and obedience to the Father's plan for reconciliation and communion.

The death of Jesus is consistent with the whole pattern of his life, a desire and a willingness to reveal the extent of God's love for all people and for them to be brought into the deepest communion of life with one another and with God. Nothing, even the prospect of violent death, would deter him from his fidelity to that mission which was given him by the Father. But the Father himself is intimately involved in this sacrificial action. He 'did not spare his own Son, but gave him up for us all' (Rom 8:32; cf 10:17f).

One cannot limit the role of the Father in the work of salvation to being the inspiration for Jesus to offer his life. Paul stresses the fact that Jesus was raised from the dead by the Father. When this is translated into the language of sacrifice it becomes nothing other than the acceptance of Jesus by the Father. Jesus died saying, 'into your hands I commend my spirit' (Lk 23:46). Resurrection is the acceptance of Jesus by the Father. It is an act of love between the Father and the Son, the mystery of self-surrender and acceptance.

The Importance of the resurrection

When one reads the accounts of the resurrection appearances of Jesus they contain many discrepancies. In Luke the appearances seem to be confined to Jerusalem and its environs, in the other gospels they are in Galilee. There are discrepancies about who went to the tomb and about what happened when they arrived there. We know that it is not the purpose of the evangelist to give us newspaper-style coverage of the events. Rather are they interested in conveying the meaning and significance of what was happening.

The situations and contexts which the evangelists describe seem to be a more fruitful way of approaching the appearances and these in turn provide important connections for us with our understanding of the Eucharist. Jesus usually appears or is seen by a number of people – there is a community dimension to the event. Even if only one is present he or she is asked to tell the others. Secondly, the message of forgiveness and reconciliation is strong in the appearance narratives. Jesus extends peace to those whom he meets and it is in the context of the post-resurrection appearances in John that he says: 'whose sins you shall forgive, they are forgiven' (20:23). Thirdly, the risen Jesus appears when the disciples are reflecting on their experiences of these last days, even as they doubted what was happening, or in the context of their attempting to understand what has happened in the light of their Jewish scriptures (see Luke 24:32). Fourthly, Jesus appears to them in the context of meals and table-fellowship: 'They recognised him at the breaking of the bread' (Lk 24:35, cf Mt 21:13-14). Fifthly, there is a recurring theme of mission in the post-resurrection appearances. Those who have had an encounter are told to go and tell the others and the parting words of Jesus at his final appearance are 'Go out to the whole world; proclaim the good news to all creation' (Mk 16:16). All of these experiences resonate with key experiences which the disciples had during the public ministry of Jesus.

The Eucharist and the church

The similarities of contexts and contents of the encounters which the disciples had before and after the resurrection event enabled them to proclaim that Jesus was alive and present among them. The community itself was for them a privileged place of encounter with the risen Jesus. So deep was their conviction about what had happened that they could no longer contain themselves but felt impelled to go out to proclaim this from the rooftops. St Luke can say that the prophetic Spirit is now poured out on the community enabling it to be the new people of God, and St Paul can speak about this same Spirit in terms of a new creation. Both of them, speaking from the experience of the early Christian community, are utterly convinced of the novelty of what has happened in the death and resurrection of Jesus. They are convinced that God's Spirit has been unleashed in a totally new and creative way, enabling the community of disciples to be the sign and anticipation of the final gathering of all God's people.

It is this community which is now the Body of Christ empowered to continue his mission in word and deed. This community is most visibly the Body of Christ when it gathers in table-fellowship to re-enact and to remember Jesus' celebration of his Last Supper with them. It is in this gathering that they understand themselves at the deepest level to be the visible sign of Christ's continuing work among his people and they are enabled to be an effective sign because of the creative-prophetic Spirit who is guiding and sustaining them.

New understanding

Gradually they were able to see the significance of what Jesus did in the Last Supper. They were able to recognise that the trust which he placed in God, as he offered his memorial, was answered, that God intervened in a new and decisive way bringing life from death and thus opening up a whole new relationship between God and the people and among the people themselves. They interpreted all of this as a new Exodus, a passage from the slavery of sin and death to freedom and new life. They say it in sacrificial terms as the offering of himself by Jesus and his total acceptance by the Father. What Jesus offered was a new Passover, a new memorial sacrificial meal. It superseded all other sacrifices which had been offered and was complete in itself. No other sacrifices were now necessary.

They began to understand their re-enactment of that last meal in terms of memorial and sacrifice. They remembered what God had done for them in the whole event of Christ's life, death and resurrection. They brought this before the people to lead them in giving thanks and praise to God for what God had done for them. They brought this before God and pleaded with God to bring this work to completion among them and among all people. Through the memorial action they were brought into contact with the original event, that foundational sacrifice which effected a new relationship between God and people. Such was the relationship between what they were doing in the re-enactment of the Supper and the original sacrifice of Christ that the only way in which they could describe what they were doing was as offering a sacrifice. However, it is not a re-offering of the original sacrifice; it is a sacramental participation in it. What makes it unique is that the same Christ who was present in the original sacrificial offering is now present in this ecclesial action as the glorified victim. He is present in the eucharistic action as a glorified body who makes himself present to the community to give it the strength it needs to be his body in every other word spoken and in every deed done by the community and its members.

This brings us to an understanding of the Eucharist which takes into account the whole paschal mystery, death and resurrection. Formerly we seemed to focus on Calvary as if there were no Easter morning. The paschal mystery is one, embracing the whole offering of his life by Christ and its acceptance by the Father. It is a genuinely ecclesial action celebrated by the church which is the Body of Christ. St Augustine said that 'the church makes the Eucharist and the Eucharist makes the church'. The truth of this insight should be clear from what has already been said. It is an action of the church before it is an action of the priest. The priest who offers Eucharist is first and foremost a member of the community and from earliest times it was because of one's leadership of the community that one was entitled to celebrate Eucharist. Hence there was the ban on absolute ordinations by the Council of Chalcedon. Because the Eucharist is a community action the one who leads it must be intimately connected with the community.

The Eucharist presupposes that the church which celebrates it is living the life of dedicated service to which it has been called by Christ, that it is a genuine community of disciples of Jesus. The Eucharist is the gathering together of all the loving, reconciling action of the community and the presenting of this, together with Christ's own great act of loving service, to the Father. Thankful for what has already been achieved, the assembly continues to intercede that this great work will soon be brought to completion.

Holy Thursday: A Living Liturgy

Siobhán Garrigan

General Guidelines

Remember to try to engage the whole person in this evening's rituals: think about how space-arrangement, visual stimuli, sound, music, touch, movement, smells, symbols and silence can be used to enable participation in the liturgy.

Environment: the atmosphere should be one of gathering to live out a story (much as Jews still do for this Passover meal), so think of how you would create the room for a family meal. For example, think about how your sanctuary is lit. Part of setting the table for a family meal involves creating a certain 'mood' through the light of lamps and candles. You can alter the 'mood' of your Eucharist in the same way by careful use of lights and candles. A warm, not too bright light, centred on the gifts on the table draws people in and makes them feel welcome.

- Use music as people enter – neither somber nor jubilant, enjoyable.
- Have greeters on the door to extend hospitality.
- Move the seats into a circle if you possibly can.

The ceremony involves plenty of symbols – place one or two in strategic points as people come in so they are in their minds (in the doorway/foyer, on the altar or in the centre of the church):

- A home-made loaf of bread symbolises the food, the meal of freedom, we are about to share. Present it on a colourful print, or with light flowers beside it to show a sense of joy at our freedom. If it is very fresh the smell will be great.
- The cross should also be prominent, as it is the symbol that links the three ceremonies of the Triduum. If you have used the ideas from Good Friday for participatory prayer crosses they will look quite effective by now.
- A symbol of service is a good indicator of the celebration to come – the jug of water, basin and towel for the feet washing could be on a stand in the entrance, or a modern day symbol of service here, like a tea cup, could be placed on a central plinth in front of the altar.

Communion should be in the form of bread and wine. Make sure you have enough chalices and eucharistic ministers. If it is not common custom in your church, explain to people how to receive the chalice so they can feel comfortable and confident doing so. You might like to use home-made unleavened bread. For a recipe, see Appendix B.

It has become accepted practice in some places to have a ritual for the renewal of commissioning of eucharistic ministers at this celebration, but this is not really appropriate. Tonight's feast is about the unity of all participants and the fact that each is equally called to serve as Jesus did. (The feast of Corpus Christi is a good alternative.)

The Gloria is often sung this evening and many places ring the bells during it. The bells are not rung again until the Easter Vigil.

Maundy Thursday is the day of the Chrism Mass in the cathedrals, when the oils are blessed by the bishops. It is good if these are then presented to the congregation in the evening – you could do this as part of the opening procession and follow it up with a short word of explanation and/or a prayer, or they could have their own procession, accompanied by special prayers for all their uses (initiation/mission/strengthening).

Tonight's liturgy revolves around two main events:
>   The washing of the feet.
>   The celebration of the Eucharist.

A Liturgy of Service
There is a motif of service running through tonight's celebration: Use of a modern-day symbol of serving one another (for example, a tea cup, a teapot, a dustpan and brush) can link several aspects of the celebration together and make them relevant/accessible to congregations.

Symbol(s) of service should be included in the opening procession and displayed prominently on a stand in the sanctuary.

Use the homily to expand on the meaning of the symbol, and the meaning of service. Here are a few notes that might be useful for preaching:
>   It is difficult to find a shared modern-day symbol of service because we no longer have a shared understanding of service.
>   Increasingly we see that those who serve us are just doing their job, for which they are paid, and therefore their 'service' becomes just another commodity.

It is with an attitude of compassion, of love, in all we do that we serve, regardless of whether it is paid or voluntary work.

It is by being Christ for one another that we serve one another.

And it is through solidarity with the poor in our community that we live out Jesus' example.

It is this solidarity in service that links the two ritual movements: the washing of the feet and the celebration of the Eucharist because this solidarity is borne in the belief that Jesus' death has liberated us from the bonds of sin, death and oppression; therefore we share a meal of hope in memory of him, as a thanksgiving.

Hold up the tea cup, or other symbol of service, as you speak.

The Washing of the Feet
Make sure you have heated the water and provided towels for drying the feet.

Ask people in advance if they will have their feet washed (not just on the night) and ask a good cross-section of the community, young and old, men and women. Explain how the ritual will take shape and exactly what is expected of them.

Think about where the feet-washing will take place so that it can be seen by all and so that it can be performed in a meaningful (not cramped) way. Use the full space of the sanctuary.

Are you going to have just the priest washing everyone's feet (takes time but is an apt symbol) or are you going to have 'couples' where each washes the other (takes less time and gives a different symbolic feel)?

Either way, the emphasis must remain on what we do for each other, not on a theatrical performance.

There is a selection of antiphons that can be sung during this time, plus a variety of hymns for solo or group singing, but the ritual is often most effective if it is performed with no singing at all. This way we all participate in the movement from awkwardness to discomfort, to the feeling of water, and finally to acceptance that one goes through when someone else washes one's feet.

The Prayers of the Faithful
These follow straight after the feet-washing. There is no creed today.

It can work well to combine the prayers with the offertory. When each prayer is said a gift is offered which symbolises the intention – for example, a loaf of bread for the hungry, Trócaire offerings for overseas development, the common cup for the lonely, etc.

The presentation of gifts focuses on those in need. If you have a project or organisation in your parish that serves those in need in a special way, include them in the writing and leadership of the prayers.

If you have prayed while the gifts are presented, one by one, you might like to arrange them on the altar prominently and sing several rounds of a chant, such as 'Ubi Caritas', as a reflection before moving on.

The Liturgy of the Eucharist
The emphasis is on God's gifts for the poor, and their liberative effect.

Make sure that gifts are offered which represent the reality of these liberative gifts in your community, and make sure they are visible to all.

Decorate the altar in such a way that it reminds us of a table set for a meal, because a meal is what this night is all about.

Use a special altar cloth, one that reflects God's gifts to your own community. For example use a cloth made by a local weaver, or a simple white cloth with lots of images (photos, etc) from your parish life pinned or sewn on. Or ask the children to make a cloth (eg. a large sheet of paper covered in paintings).

The cloth could be processed up to the sanctuary and the table 'laid' as the other gifts are offered. Involve as many people as possible in the offertory and the decoration of the altar. The decoration is a great task for older children.

Our unity with the poor is symbolised in the one bread, one cup. Using homemade bread on this night can deepen our understanding of this central symbol, but it is important to gauge the size of loaf well.

It is good to include children in the Eucharist – they could gather around all sides of the altar for the Eucharistic Prayer, so they can see the bread and wine, and the priest could ask them to hold up the elements when they are being blessed.

After communion, the Sacrament is taken to the place of reservation in a simple, dignified procession, usually accompanied by congregational singing. There follows a period of silent adoration, after which the priests and ministers leave in silence.

The altar is stripped, and the crosses removed or covered.

All are encouraged to watch and pray for an hour of the evening – until midnight. Some parishes organise this street by street, area by area, while others leave it random.

In some churches, there is a prayer board in a side chapel and during the watch people can write their petitions and leave them pinned to the board.

Other churches organise a holy hour during this time, but the emphasis should remain on individual prayer.

Holy Thursday: Further Suggestions

Patricia Lynott

General Comments

Creating liturgy is exciting because it allows us to explore all kinds of possibilities! Yet it can be difficult to really push boundaries and look at possibilities because naturally we are aware of our own communities, our own churches, the amount of space, etc. Sometimes, in order to create a meaningful liturgy, we have to explore outside of what seems possible, we have to dare to dream and then, as the saying goes, 'Cut your cloth according to your measure!'

Another point worth mentioning is the tendency at times, to overload the liturgy. We have so many ideas, we are so enthusiastic. We want as much participation as possible from the congregation. *Active participation* is important but it's good to remember that active participation also includes a strong *inner participation.*

It's not so much about 'what can I use to make the liturgy different?' as 'how can I bring new life to the familiar?' Therefore it's helpful to spend time reflecting on the Word of God for Holy Thursday … prayerfully pondering… allowing the Spirit to move us to action.

I feel it's helpful to have a main peg around which we create our liturgy.

1. Our focus could be to create a sense of gathering to live out the story: 1 Cor 11:23-27: 'Do this in memory of me.'
- Highlighting the gift of Christ's Body and Blood
- Appreciating the Eucharist
- Re-calling, re-enacting the Last Supper.

How can we best create an environment which will allow and enable inner participation and free movement of the Spirit?

Through the use of symbols:
  Sheaf of wheat
  Flour
  Bread
  Large bunches of grapes
  Decanter of wine/
  Wine poured out in a glass
All nicely displayed in front of and around the altar.

I'm emphasising *big* so that people can actually see or at least get a sense of what is there lest it become a distraction rather than an aid to liturgy.

Alternatively, have the symbols carried in the entrance procession, holding each symbol high and then placed.

Offertory Procession
If Eucharist, re-calling, re-enacting the Last Supper, is the focus, I think it could be meaningful to have people come forward to prepare the altar.

Gather from different parts of the church carrying:
  Altar cloth
  Corporal

Flowers
Candles.

Allow time to have the altar prepared and then have the bread and wine carried in procession to the altar.

It gives time to move the focus of the liturgy.

An alternative
✓ Combined Offertory procession and prayers
Baskets of Trócaire Boxes … Prayer
Chrism oils … Prayer
Bread … Prayer
Wine … Prayer

✓ What about the people involved in the procession staying around the altar until the Sign of Peace and then taking the Sign of Peace to the congregation and going back to their places?

Homily
Focus in on Eucharist – What it was like for Jesus to celebrate the Last Supper.

2. Perhaps the main focus could be: Service born out of love. The dignity of the work of our human hands … highlighting the mutuality of service…

Entrance Procession
People carrying symbols of their work/areas of service. Anything from a 'j cloth' to a fishing rod, a fireman's hat to a teacher's chalk. All of these can form part of a display around the altar.

or

Choose just one symbol to be carried in the Offertory Procession ... One that crosses boundaries ... Evokes memories ... Speaks to all people in some way ... A cup and saucer comes to my mind ... It speaks to me of fellowship, love, companionship, giving, receiving ... It links the cup of everyday with the shared cup of the Eucharist. It could be meaningful if the priest at homily time focuses in on the cup and saucer and the whole idea of the mutuality of service.

Washing of the feet

The washing of the feet is not simply re-enacting what happened at the Last Supper, it is an act of humble service. If we are focusing on the mutuality of service, could it be possible to have people in little groups washing each other's feet? The priest included.

It would be good to use all of the sanctuary space or areas around the church.

Allow people to come from their places rather than from neatly organised rows in seats, as long as it doesn't cause an unnecessary delay and disrupt the flow of the liturgy. A suitable hymn could be sung as the place is being prepared. As the washing takes place there may be no need for music or song, simply allow the people the freedom to look around at what is happening and to hear the sound of the water. During the clearing away, a suitable hymn could be sung.

Concluding Rite
Simple procession to the altar of repose.
Atmosphere of quiet reverence.

Stripping done then or later?

Sometimes I wonder about the mood of the atmosphere at this time. I envisage there being even a little consternation at the time ... fear ... questioning ... cry for understanding.

I found this mood very beautifully and powerfully captured with an ecumenical setting, where immediately after Eucharist there was a very short dramatisation of Jesus in the garden. (Another area within the church could be used or alternatively move outside the church.) Followed by the arrest of Jesus. This can be done very simply through the use of strong voices, shouts, clamour of feet, changes in lighting.

Meanwhile a rather hurried stripping of the altar is taking place. All combined to create a meaningful experience.

It was after the evening worship on Good Friday that we met for some silent and some communal prayer. We gathered in four different areas ... one area represented the men who fled ... another the women who went to the tomb ... another the different churches ... and another represented the different nations.

Although the prayer was the same, the fact that the congregation was split up highlighted the feeling of confusion and witnessed to the dispersion of the people after the death of Jesus.

Holy Thursday: Suggested Music

Francis McMyler

Entrance:
Gathering Hymn
or
Though so many we are one
(*Jean Paul Lécot, Alleluia Amen 79*)

Psalm:
The Blessing Cup
(*Marty Haugen, Psalms for the Church Year, Vol 1*)

Washing the feet:
The Lord Jesus (*Gregory Norbert OSB, Alleluia Amen 82*)

Presentation of the Gifts:
Ubi Caritas (*Music from Taizé, Vol 1*)

Memorial Acclamation:
When we eat this bread (*Alleluia Amen 18*)

Amen:
(*Jean Paul Lécot, Mass of Our Lady of Lourdes*)

Lamb of God:
(*Lucien Deiss, Mass of Our Lady of Lourdes*)

Holy Communion:
Take and eat (*Michael Joncas, Hosanna 216*)
or
Take this and eat it

Procession:
Ubi Caritas (*Music from Taizé, Vol 1*)
Pange Lingua (*Holy Ghost Hymnal*)

Good Friday

First Reading, Isaiah 52:13 - 53:12,
arranged for reading in parts

Voice 1:   See, my servant will prosper,
            he shall be lifted up, exalted, rise to great
            heights.

Voice 2:   As the crowds were appalled on seeing him,
            – so disfigured did he look
            that he seemed no longer human –
            so will the crowds be astonished at him,
            and kings stand speechless before him;
            for they shall see something never told
            and witness something never heard before:
            'Who could believe what we have heard,
            and to whom has the power of the Lord been
            revealed?'

Voice 3:   Like a sapling he grew up in front of us,
            like a root in arid ground.
            Without beauty, without majesty (we saw him),
            no looks to attract our eyes:
            a thing despised and rejected by men,
            a man of sorrows and familiar with suffering,
            a man to make people screen their faces.

All: He was despised and we took no account of
              him.

Voice 3:   And yet ours were the sufferings he bore,
              ours the sorrows he carried.
              But we, we thought of him as someone
              punished,
              struck by God and brought low.
              Yet he was pierced through for our faults,
              crushed for our sins.

All: On him lies a punishment that brings us peace,
              and through his wounds we are healed.

Voice 3:   We had all gone astray like sheep,
              each taking his own way,
              and the Lord burdened him
              with the sins of all of us.

Voice 2:   Harshly dealt with, he bore it humbly,
              he never opened his mouth,
              like a lamb that is led to the slaughter-house,
              like a sheep that is dumb before his shearers
              never opening his mouth.

              By force and by law he was taken;
              would anyone plead his cause?
              Yes, he was torn away from the land of the
              living;
              for our faults struck down in death.
              They gave him a grave with the wicked,
              a tomb with the rich,
              though he had done no wrong
              and there had been no purjury in his mouth.

The Lord has been pleased to crush him with
suffering.
If he offers his life in atonement,
he shall see his heirs, he shall have a long life
and through him what the Lord wishes will be
done.

Voice 1:   His soul's anguish over
he shall see the light and be content.
By his sufferings shall my servant justify
many,
taking their faults on himself.

Hence I will grant whole hoards for his tribute,
he shall divide the spoil with the mighty,
for surrendering himself to death
and letting himself be taken for a sinner,
while he was bearing the faults of many
and praying all the time for sinners.

Recipe for Unleavened Bread

Mix together:
– Two cups of wholemeal flour
– One tablespoon of cooking oil
– Half a teaspoon of salt
– Enough warm water to mix to a smooth dough

Leave to rest for at least half an hour, wrapped in cling film.

Then take small portions (egg-sized) and roll out thinly on a floured board to about the size of a side plate.

Place under a hot grill till the cakes blister – approximately 2 to 3 minutes.

Turn and grill the other side and they are ready.

If no grill is available, they can be cooked in a very hot oven.

The Contributors

EUGENE DUFFY is a theologian and priest of the diocese of Achonry. He is Director of The Western Theological Institute, Galway.

SIOBHAN GARRIGAN is a theologian and liturgist. She lives in Westport, Co Mayo.

CELIA HAYES is a native of Bunclody, Co Wexford. She is a catechist currently working in Salerno Secondary Scool, Galway. She also works with the chaplaincy team in the Galway Mayo Institute of Technology.

PATRICIA LYNOTT is a religious of Jesus and Mary, based in Gortnor Abbey, Crossmolina, Co Mayo. She is presently working as a Diocesan Adviser for Religious Education in the diocese of Killala.

ENDA LYONS is a theologian and priest of the diocese of Tuam. He is author of *Partnership in Parish* (Columba Press, 1987) and *Jesus Self-Portrait by God* (Columba Press, 1994).

FRANCIS MCMYLER, a priest of the diocese of Tuam, is Parish Priest of Balla, Co Mayo.